NO SACRED GROUND

"HUMAN RIGHTS" THOUGHT POLICE CLAMPING DOWN ON CHRISTIANS

TIMOTHY BLOEDOW

Published by
Bloedow, Timothy
Printed in the United States of America

ISBN 978-0-9782942-2-9

First Edition

TABLE OF CONTENTS

INTRODUCTION

The Ontario Human Rights Tribunal decision in April 2008 against Christian Horizons has horrified many Christians. This was an incredibly dangerous decision that now puts churches directly in the line of fire of the well-trained "human rights" militants! In some respects, it wasn't a surprising decision in view of current trends. In this case, the agents of the government have again applied principles that they have been implementing for a number of years to push Christians into the closet and to steal our fundamental freedoms from us. But this case is a significant example of how Canada's socialist Establishment incrementally builds on its successes in order to pursue its socialist/state-ist vision for this country. Other than an outright ban on Christianity, there isn't much more these thugs can do to marginalize Christians other than to revoke the charitable tax status of churches, and to repeal previous promises that clergy would be off-limits to the "Human Rights" Machine.

Let's look quickly at what happened. Then we need to dig in to the serious implications of this decision – we will explore nine different aspects of this HRC decision against Christian

Horizons. Finally we need to think about what we must do to fight back.

Who decided to target Christian Horizons?

In their own words, Christian Horizons is a non-profit, Christian charitable organization that seeks to reach out with supports and friendship to persons who have exceptional needs. Their purpose is to contribute to the exceptional person's quality of life by addressing his/her spiritual, emotional, intellectual, social and physical needs. They serve in a manner that considers each person's intrinsic value as loved by God and bearing His image. Christian Horizons is Ontario's largest provider of developmental services. They offer services for persons with disabilities in Canada and globally. Their services also include professional training opportunities and resources for churches interested in inclusion programs for the disabled.

I will briefly summarize the events that led up to the filing of the complaint against Christian Horizons from the material found in the Ontario Human Rights Tribunal decision itself.

A former employee, Ms. Connie Heintz, filed a complaint against Christian Horizons with the Ontario Human Rights Commission. She was accusing them of violating her human rights by discriminating against her on the basis of her "sexual orientation." She resigned from Christian Horizons in the face of pressure to do so after the organisation learnt that she was living with another woman in a lesbian relationship.

Christian Horizons requires its employees to affirm a Statement of Faith and a code of conduct, or "Lifestyle and Morality Statement." It is an Evangelical organization and the

Lifestyle and Morality Statement insists that its employees refrain from a number of sinful and unhelpful behaviours and activities. These include adultery, engaging in pre-marital sex, homosexual relationships, theft, fraud, sexual harassment, using pornography and illicit drugs.

The Kitchener Record reported that Christian Horizons also bans employees from using alcohol and tobacco. I'm not sure where they drew that information from. It's not in the list of banned activities given in paragraph 68 of the OHRC decision, which looks like it was cut and pasted directly from a Christian Horizons document. Perhaps the *Record* wanted to use these items of lesser moral significance – while ignoring the references to sexual assault and fraud – to make Christian Horizons' moral position seem petty and absurd to a larger number of people. I suspect that many more people would see Christian Horizons as reasonable if they knew they took a stand against sexual assault, whereas dogmatic opposition to alcohol tends to marginalize people in today's society. I suppose this is another example of objective, honest reporting from Canada's mainstream media! (Mercer, 2008)

Ms. Heintz was accepted as an employee in 1995 at which time she signed Christian Horizons' Lifestyle and Morality Statement. By 1999, she started to explore lesbian temptations and soon began living with another woman in a lesbian relationship. During that time, she told two co-workers about her interest in lesbianism or, to use the deferential language in the OHRC decision, "she confided with two of her co-workers about **her new awareness of her sexual orientation**" (emphasis added).

Soon after, Ms. Heintz's supervisor, Ms. Dorothy Girling, confronted her and asked if she was in a same-sex relationship.

Ms. Heintz did not deny her relationship and her sexual orientation. This encounter prompted a series of events that ultimately resulted in Ms. Heintz resigning her employment with Christian Horizons in September 2000.

During this time, "Ms. Heintz was offered counseling in her Evangelical tradition to assist her in determining whether she could return to compliance with the basic requirements of her employment. Instead, she resigned, filing a human rights complaint four months later." (Hutchinson, 2008)

Several months later, in January 2001, Ms. Heintz filed her complaint against Christian Horizons with the Ontario Human Rights Commission (OHRC). Three and a half years later, on June 21, 2005, the Commission referred the complaint to the Ontario Human Rights Tribunal (OHRT) for adjudication.

In numerous places, the OHRT decision demonstrates prejudicial favouritism towards Ms. Heintz over Christian Horizons. It refers to Ms. Heintz as a woman of "deep faith," and it records that Ms. Heintz "came to terms with" her sexual orientation as a lesbian and that she "began to develop an awareness of her sexual orientation." On the other hand, when writing about Christian Horizons, the adjudicator records that "Christian Horizons **identifies** as a religious organization," that it "**self-identifies** as an Evangelical Christian ministry," that "**[i]t considers** its work [to be] Christian ministry," and that they "live out **what they perceive** as a Biblical mandate …" (emphases added).

When talking about Ms. Heintz, however, the adjudicator doesn't say that she "believes" she's a lesbian, or that it's her "sincere belief" that she's a lesbian, or that she simply "self-identifies" as a lesbian. The militant prejudice and homosexualized bigotry is palpable. This attitude reflected in the decision is also incompatible with the tone and posture of a serious court decision, illustrating the incompatibility of human rights commissions with a civilized, free and just society.

Further in the decision, the OHRT records in quotation marks Ms. Heintz's supervisor's comment about the employee's need to bring herself in line with the Lifestyle and Morality Statement as being "a matter of integrity." By doing so, the Tribunal sends the message that a person's failure to honour their word by way of a contractual agreement is not necessarily a matter of integrity. As we learn throughout this decision – and other cultural developments with which it is consistent – such people see integrity as involving the total acceptance, affirmation, endorsement and celebration of homosexual behaviour. Anything that gets in the way of this slavish veneration of sexual activity is seen as an assault on integrity, human dignity and self-esteem.

What did the Ontario Human Rights Commission do?

The short answer is that they ruled against Christian Horizons – and in so doing, they poured out their contempt on Christianity, demonstrating the dangerous implications of allowing Secular Humanism to remain Ontario's official religion.

The key components of this decision are that:
- Christian Horizons was found guilty of discrimination on the basis of "sexual orientation;"
- Christian Horizons has been ordered to pay Connie Heintz $23,000, plus interest as well as any wages and benefits she would have received in the 18-month period after she left the organization;
- The $23,000 includes $5,000 for "the willful and reckless

infliction of mental anguish, $8,000 for the application of a discriminatory employment policy and $10,000 for a poisoned work environment;"
- Christian Horizons must stop imposing the Lifestyle and Morality Statement as a condition of employment;
- Christian Horizons must develop and adopt anti-discrimination and anti-harassment policies as well as a human rights training program for all employees and managers;
- Christian Horizons must adopt an anti-discrimination and anti-harassment policy.

A more accurate way to summarize this decision is that:
- It asserts that Christianity isn't fundamental to Christian Horizons' service;
- It treats sexual behaviour as a greater value than religious liberty;
- It deprives Christian Horizons of freedom of thought by requiring the organization to indoctrinate its employees in the state's offensive ideology;
- It requires Christian Horizons to impose a workplace ethic that is hostile to the organization's Christian values;
- It violates the freedom to exercise voluntary binding contracts;
- It leaves Christian Horizons' disabled clients more vulnerable to inadequate and even predatory caregivers by preventing the organization from screening its potential employees according to fundamental criteria.

There are many particulars in this 73-page decision that deserve consideration, but only the most relevant aspects will be addressed here. The OHRC's one-page press release highlights the priority issues as the Tribunal and Commission see them, so the points they have chosen to emphasise in their anti-Christian decision will be important to the analysis that follows.

Following is the text of the OHRT press release:

April 25, 2008

TRIBUNAL RULES ON EMPLOYEE LIFESTYLE AND MORALITY STATEMENT

The Human Rights Tribunal of Ontario released its decision in the case of Connie Heintz v. Christian Horizons. The decision has a significant impact for faith-based and other organizations that provide services to the general public. Such organizations must ensure their hiring policies and practices do not unreasonably restrict or exclude the employment of persons based on grounds under the Ontario Human Rights Code.

Ms. Heintz, an individual of deep Christian faith, and a model employee for five years with Christian Horizons, was providing care and support to individuals with developmental disabilities. Like other employees, when first hired, Ms. Heintz was required to sign a Lifestyle and Morality Statement, which prohibits, among other things, homosexual relationships. After several years, Ms. Heintz came to terms with her sexual orientation as a lesbian. When Christian Horizons discovered this, they advised her that she was not complying with the Statement and required her to leave the organization.

Christian Horizons describes itself as an Evangelical Christian Ministry that provides care and residential services to 1,400 developmentally disabled individuals of all races, creeds and sexual orientations. With over 180 residential homes across Ontario, and 2,500 employees, Christian Horizons is the largest provider of community living services in the province, funded almost exclusively by the Ontario Ministry of Community and Social Services.

The Tribunal ruled that Christian Horizons could not require its employees to sign the Statement. It found that Christian Horizons is primarily engaged in serving the disability-related needs of its clients, and the prohibition on homosexual relationships was not a legitimate job requirement for providing quality care and support to disabled residents.

In addition to awarding Ms. Heintz lost wages, general damages and damages for mental anguish, the decision sets out that Christian Horizons will: no longer require employees to sign a lifestyle and morality statement; develop anti-discrimination policies; provide training to all employees and managers; and review all of its employment policies to ensure that they are in compliance with the Code.

"This decision is important," commented Chief Commissioner Barbara Hall, "because it sets out that when faith-based and other organizations move beyond serving the interests of their particular community to serving the general public, the rights of others, including employees, must be respected."

This is yet another case which pitted Christianity against homosexuality. The HRT analysis essentially sought to determine "how homosexual" Connie Heintz was and "how Christian," Christian Horizons was, and whether Christian Horizon's Christianity was more important than Ms. Heintz's homosexuality, or vice versa. "For Christian Horizons, this case goes to its very identity and existence. … For Ms. Heintz, this case is equally fundamental. It is tied to her identity and dignity, to her sexuality, to her sense as a person of faith," reads the decision.

As usual – and notwithstanding the Tribunal's dutiful yet dishonest assertion that "it has been said that no right is absolute" – the fundamentalist HRT adjudicator, Michael Gottheil, decided that homosexuality was more important than Christianity and, therefore, in this case, that sexual expression was more important than those Christian Horizons clients who are being treated as annoying, funny-looking cripples who should be seen and not heard. Such is the cruel and uncivilized nature of Canada's fundamentalist pro-homosexual religion of Secular Humanism.

Ms. Heintz could demonstrate that her complaint against Christian Horizons was not simply an ignorant, selfish and disgusting attempt to grab some "free money" at the expense of a bunch of "retards" by announcing her commitment to donate 100 percent of the money the OHRT awarded her back to Christian Horizons or to another ministry that serves vulnerable Canadians. I'll believe it when I see it!

Technically speaking, the Tribunal probably had to rule the way it did because the OHRC and the OHRT exist to implement and adjudicate the Ontario Human Rights Act, and this piece of legislation stipulates that the provincial human rights code trumps voluntary contracts signed between employers and employees. This shouldn't be, and the situation is an example of the many systemic problems with the human rights operation that warrant the complete abolition of the industry. And despite this situation, the fact that this decision does trump voluntary contractual agreements warrants discussion and is the first point of dispute I address below.

Another technical matter is the fact that the only way Christian Horizons could have won a positive decision from the Tribunal would have been if the adjudicator agreed to recognize it as an exempt organization governed by "'special employment' provisions:"

> [6] Christian Horizons argues that it falls within the "special employment" provisions of section 24(1)(a) of the *Human Rights Code*, which permits certain organizations to restrict hiring or give preference in employment to persons identified by one of the proscribed grounds of discrimination, in this case, creed. It submits that strict adherence to its articles of faith, Doctrinal Statement and Lifestyle and Morality Statement is a reasonable and *bona fide* qualification given the nature of the employment. ...

Clearly the OHRT did not agree with Christian Horizons in this respect. In view of this, fact, this is a vital decision, which has dangerous totalitarian tendencies, and warrants serious examination.

Christian Horizons has announced its response to the decision. It will appeal most of the ruling, but it will comply with the order not to require its employees to sign their Lifestyle and Morality Statement.

How much does Ontario hate Christians? Let us count the ways...

This decision by the OHRT against Christian Horizons, the reasons given for it, and some of the commentary and opinion available from politicians, journalists and other citizens, demonstrates how fragile Canadian society is today. I am going to explore nine important points of controversy between Christians and Canada's secular humanist Establishment – points that reflect the growing totalitarian tendencies among Canada's left-wing ideologues. The human rights commissions are the "Shock Troops" of Canada's Fundamentalist-Left, and they are leaving no stone unturned in their attempt to surgically remove every evidence of Christianity from Canada's public square.

CHAPTER ONE

VIOLATION OF PRIVATE CONTRACTUAL AGREEMENTS

Let's look first at one aspect of the ruling that will unite all clear-thinking Christians, conservatives and libertarians in criticism of this "human rights" decision; namely, the disregard given to the voluntary contractual agreement that employee Connie Heintz made with employer Christian Horizons.

Practically speaking, this interference by the OHRT as an agent of the state in the voluntary contractual agreement between Ms. Heintz and Christian Horizons suggests that Ms. Heintz was such a pathetic, weak individual that she should not be expected to honour her word. This is the implication written into the human rights code for most complainants. "The Human Rights Code is a quasi-constitutional statute. Its provisions prevail over other provincial laws and over private employment contracts," recorded Michael Gottheil, the adjudicator to whom the writing of the decision is attributed.

This fact exposes the human rights code as inherently incompatible with a society committed to liberty and equity. It's a tragedy that Ontarians, and the rest of the country, have allowed it to survive for so many decades.

The state should have no right to interfere in private contracts unless a law has been broken, such as if the contract involved killing someone or if any of the terms were suspected as being fraudulent. But, some will respond, the HR Code is law, so it is against the law to violate "human rights" in voluntary contracts. This challenge requires one to take sides as to whose ethical system is superior. Without a doubt, the Christian liberty ethic is superior to the suffocating state-ism and group rights mentality of the "human rights" ethic. Ayn Rand, a thorough-going atheist, but one strongly supportive of individual liberty, summed up the fascist nature of the corrupt state poignantly when she wrote: "There's no way to rule innocent men. The only power government has is the power to crack down on criminals. Well, when there aren't enough criminals, one makes them. One declares so many things to be a crime that it becomes impossible for men to live without breaking laws." Such is the totalitarian nature of Canada's "human rights" industry.

Interestingly, the same week that the Christian Horizons decision was announced, an activist Montreal judge ruled in a case involving a 33-year-old Mohawk defendant that the Aboriginal offender should get special treatment because he was an Indian. Her rationale falls along the same affirmative action lines that form the foundation of today's Establishment thinking about homosexuality. Announcing his release, the judge said, "We have to take into account the fact you are a native American." She also said aboriginals are "disadvantaged in our society, and that is sometimes shown by the heavy rate of underemployment and alcohol," as reported by Margaret Wente in the Globe and Mail. (Wente, 2008)

Equality-affirming Aboriginals such as Rhonda Kirby, a chief who sits on the Mohawk Council of Kahnawake, were disgusted at the judge's patronising attitude. She said that "if he's guilty he should be treated as guilty. I think it was a bit racist for the judge to be making comments like that." Grand Chief Mike Delisle also condemned the decision: "It's a slap in the face. It's saying, 'They're poor little Indians.'" (Wente, 2008)

So, where are the homosexual activists condemning the "poor little Indian" mentality articulated by OHRT adjudicator Michael Gottheil in his decision against Christian Horizons? The silence is deafening – as it always is from Canadian homosexual activists who treasure the Billy club power that today's legislative environment gives them to beat their Christian enemies into subjection.

And one of the benefits of this "poor little Indian" mentality is that those deemed to be victims of a cruel and backward culture are not expected to honour their word, keep their vows or respect contracts they voluntarily signed.

Trust and honour are foundational

Trust is foundational to a stable society, whether we are talking about the simple trust experienced in friendship, the expectation that people will honour their word in business arrangements, or the confidence we have that we can walk down the street without being indiscriminately attacked.

This trust has been eroding in Western society for several decades now and the situation is only getting worse. We see it in the rising rates of violent crime, in the lack of commitment in our justice system to effectively combat perjury, in the equality-hating affirmative action provisions that trump voluntary contractual financial agreements, and most destructively, in Canada's tacit acceptance of the late Liberal Prime Minister Pierre Trudeau's implementation of "no fault" divorce.

In fact, due to the centrality of marriage and the family unit in the economy of God, marriage is the most important contract and set of vows that people make to each other. As a result, when a country's laws and when its cultural and moral norms no longer act to buttress people's marriage vows, such developments must impact the way people approach any and all their other contracts, promises and agreements. This doesn't bring society crashing down overnight, but it sows the seeds for the decline of honour, trust, civility and, therefore, social peace.

One of the outcomes of this contract-breaking mentality, along with other forces that we will explore below, is today's situation where people designated as belonging to a victim class are not required by law to honour their contracts. Furthermore, civil government authorities reserve the right to retroactively change the nature of agreements, requiring the "systemic oppressors" – the employers – to cover whatever costs may arise from the HRC decision.

According to testimony in the OHRT decision, when Christian Horizons first implemented the Lifestyle and Morality Statement, "between 5 and 12 employees felt they could not sign the new contract, and left their employment with Christian Horizons." This is what free conscientious people do. But thugs look around for a baseball bat, such as a human rights commission, with which to use to assault their (former) employer.

All people concerned about social and economic stability must be concerned about this deeply disturbing situation. It's very troubling, therefore, that we don't see a broad cross-section of people rallying against these kinds of decisions. It's not as though the ruling against Christian Horizons is the first of its kind, notwithstanding the particular aspects of this decision that make it especially ominous. The reality is, however, that the general public is radically homophobic (terrified of homosexual activists) and also fearful of getting mired in "religious" (read "Christian") controversies, and their apathy and fear allows this kind of secular humanist corruption to fester and to grow.

Even the valiant freedom fighter and provocative conservative commentator, Ezra Levant, has not yet discussed the Christian Horizons case on his website. His blog is one of the best archives and running commentaries on the crackpot industry of human rights commissions since he started it in January 2008 to report on his own case in Alberta. Mr. Levant is on top of most cases and developments, reporting on many of them within a day or two of the latest absurd decision from one province or another.

It seems that Christians are on their own when it comes to defending the honour of God, the foundational freedoms that Christians should be able to enjoy and the Christian ethics that form the foundation of civilised society for all people. Perhaps that is as it should be. Yet, it's disappointing to see this huge blind spot in the vision of those whose underlying philosophical principles suggest that they should be supporters of a similar vision for the renewal of our culture.

CHAPTER TWO

THE SOCIALIST TRIBUNAL IMPOSES A RIGHT TO EMPLOYMENT

Another economic aspect of the decision against Christian Horizons that should unite social and economic conservatives against this absurd ruling is its implication that a person has a right to employment – and a right to a particular employer.

The adjudicator ruled that Christian Horizons violated Ms. Heintz's basic human rights by requiring her to comply with their Lifestyle and Morality Statement while employed there. He also ruled that the Statement violates the human rights of all the employees. This is a bizarre decision that defies reason. Christian Horizons is not telling these employees that they have to abide by their Lifestyle and Morality Statement for the rest of their lives. They are not putting a gun to their employees' heads, to force compliance to this Statement even while they are employed there. They are simply saying that **if** they want to work at Christian Horizons, then while they are working there, they are expected to comply with this Lifestyle and Morality Statement.

Christian Horizons is not saying that a person has to sign the Statement in order to walk down the sidewalk past one of their group homes. They are not saying that a person has to sign the Statement in order to work for a company located next door to a Christian Horizons group home. They are not saying that a person has to sign the Statement in order to have a personal relationship with a Christian Horizons employee. You are only expected to sign it if you are accepted as an employee with the organization.

Christian Horizons is demonstrating the principle of individual liberty: freedom of choice. Michael Gottheil, the adjudicator, on the other hand, has become the freedom-crushing Enforcer by condemning Christian Horizons from attracting the kind of employees they want and the kind of employees they think would be best for the quality of care they want to give to their disabled clients.

Alexander McQuire from Cambridge, Ontario, wrote to the *Waterloo Region Record* supporting this notion that somehow people have the right to work where they choose and that the state should have the authority to force this expectation on the province's employers:

> The recent situation where Christian Horizons received a rebuke ensures that basic human rights are established in the land for all individuals. It is right and proper that standards of behaviour are established and broadly accepted throughout our civil society, for that makes it civil. However, when policies, standards and codes are discriminatory, dictatorial and invasive and attempt to reach into an individual's private life, when that

individual has committed no crime, then they have no place in our democracy. The essence of democracy is the lone individual, protected and defended by law, against all injustice perpetrated by another individual, group or government. (McQuire, 2008)

Mr. McQuire's notion of democracy allows for the civil government to impose its will on every facet of society. That used to be called dictatorship. His view doesn't impose expectations on employees to exercise their freedom of choice to work or live in an environment that is conducive to their own values and priorities! Mr. McQuire is possessed of the group rights and class warfare notion of social victims and oppressors, and the need for the state to represent the politically-defined victims. (There's no commitment to the principle of equality before the law here.) Mr. McQuire is an advocate of socialist tyranny and oppression, not of democratic liberty.

The underlying assumption of Mr. Gottheil's decision – if there's any rational basis for it at all – is that Ms. Heintz has a legally enforceable right to work, and not just a general right to work, but a right to work at Christian Horizons – as though once she expressed her right to work there, they had to accept her as an employee. And then they had to keep her on as an employee as long as **SHE** chose to work there. Such an approach to employment, or to social order in general, is wholly incompatible with the principles of democratic liberty.

The heart of the matter is that Christian Horizons' Lifestyle and Morality Statement doesn't conform to the sex worship that is central to the public policy priorities of Canada's politicians and cultural leaders – a pre-civilized ethic that celebrates almost every expression of sexual permissiveness and "diversity." Specifically – yet again – the sanction against homosexuality was the source of this conflict with Christian Horizons.

It is true that in the early 1990s, Christian Horizons faced a challenge from a couple they fired because they were living in a common-law relationship. In this case, the Human Rights Board of Inquiry, the predecessor to the Ontario Human Rights Commission, in 1992 found Christian Horizons guilty of discrimination and fined them $65,000.

In most cases, however, regardless of the various moral restrictions included in a Christian code of conduct, it is the ban on homosexual behaviour that becomes the point of conflict. This may be due to a particular level of self-absorption, rebellion or hatred against Christians that exists among those committed to homosexual behaviour. Or it could be due to the special status and rights that exist in Canadian law and culture today for homosexuals, which doesn't exist for adulterers, fornicators, consumers of pornography, pot smokers or drunks (to reference other examples of unwelcome behaviour listed in Christian Horizon's Lifestyle and Morality Statement). If that inequality and advantage in the law exists to attain free money and more power, then why not use it to advance one's own rights and benefits? That's the rational, self-interested thing to do. Such foolishness highlights why the uniquely Judeo-Christian principle of equality before the law is so essential to the long-term survival of a civilization – and why the abandonment of this principle in Canada and other Western nations today is such a threat to our social peace and ordered liberty.

Whatever the reason, these actions and precedents reflect fundamental principles that ultimately impact all people, not just Christians. This imposition of a right to work that essentially gives agents of the civil government the right to impose retroactive punitive measures against businesses is a case in point. This right exists not in the face of any criminal wrong-doing by the business, but because of the civil government's interest in imposing a particular "social" vision on the country – a vision that must be imposed because ordinary Canadians would not freely move in the desired direction.

In relation to this observation, it's worth noting a comment made by columnist Mark Steyn on a recent episode of CTV's Mike Duffy Live. In April, the Ontario Human Rights Commission ruled that they didn't have the jurisdiction to prosecute *Maclean's* magazine for its publication of portions of Mr Steyn's book, "America Alone." Nevertheless, in the announcement, chief commissioner Barbara Hall lashed out with a blistering condemnation of *Maclean's* and Mark Steyn's writing. In her diatribe, to put Mr. Steyn's accurate spin on her words, she indicated that "she thinks Ontarians essentially aren't being hateful enough so we need to define hate crimes more loosely to enable her to whip up a bit of business." Canadians aren't hate mongers so they don't need HR Codes to beat them into civilised human beings. Therefore the HRCs justify their existence by stirring up trouble and targeting political victims.

Another example of the purely ideological nature of this case is the acknowledgement that Ms. Heintz has no interest in returning to work for Christian Horizons. So what then is the point of the case? To exact revenge on Christians Horizons and to exercise their Messianic complexes by supposedly keeping the organisation from violating any other employee's "human rights." Ms. Heintz and the Ontario Human Rights commissioners and adjudicators show absolutely no compassion or concern for the dignity and well-being of the vulnerable disabled clients served by Christian Horizons. This is a purist ideological exercise by secular humanist fundamentalists.

The agenda of the Ontario Human Rights Commission is one of social engineering – radically transforming Canada into a socialist tyranny – a state-ist dictatorship – that has banned fundamental personal liberties. Broadly speaking, they and other cultural leaders are trying to move Canada from a Christian ethos rooted in the Ten Commandments to the morally bankrupt ethical model of "human rights." Today's human rights paradigm is one of group rights and class warfare, affirmative action, parity of outcome and suffocating state control over every area of life that encompasses charity, economics and family life.

Even basic economic liberties will be a thing of the past if this trend continues. The outcome we see with the Christian Horizons case will be replicated again and again. The terms of a contract are enforced, not on the basis of their own terms, but at the whim of the state. Businesses are effectively nationalized as civil magistrates exercise a prerogative even in setting the terms of employment – retroactively if necessary. It's sad that when homosexual activism is a component of such trends, self-professed libertarians and "economic conservatives" lack the insight to see what's going on and the courage to confront these dangerous forces. It seems as though it is left to Christians to fight for the survival of Canadian civilization – for everybody.

CHAPTER THREE

SO WHAT IF CHRISTIAN HORIZONS IS INCONSISTENT

Some people have said that Christian Horizons isn't consistent in applying its Code of Conduct. That could be a problem in view of the ideological bent of today's laws, courts and "human rights" commissions, but at the end of the day, that should be Christian Horizon's business. If any employees don't like it, they can try to find a rationale for launching a lawsuit against them, but the fact is that Christian Horizons is running the show because they are the employer, so they should have the right to apply their principles as they see fit. If an employee doesn't like it, he can go and find work somewhere else. If Christian Horizons applies its principles in a way that lacks integrity, then in a free society, word of such behaviour will leak out and will impact their effectiveness at attracting quality employees. This will undermine their operation, so they will be forced to shape up or face closure. That's an example of the freedom oriented, Christian approach to dealing with employer-employee disputes. It assumes adult-level maturity among the parties. It is very different from the oppressive socialist paternalism practised by today's "human rights" regime.

The reality is that when you are dealing with employees, you are dealing with human beings with all kinds of individual situations. This means that even if you have a Code of Conduct that you call employees to respect, you may want the freedom to exercise some charitable flexibility when implementing it. This being the case, a) you are not always going to make the right decision, and b) your decisions are not always going to be understood by third-party observers who are unaware of all the details that led you to your final decision.

Whatever the truth may or may not be regarding the consistency of Christian Horizons' application of their own rules to employee retention, that is their business. Civil governments have no business interfering in these decisions and second-guessing them.

Jesus Christ told his listeners a parable one day (Matthew 20:1-16) about a landowner who hired various temporary labourers at different times throughout the day. He hired some at the beginning of the day with an agreement to pay them a particular wage for the day's work, and he hired others later, apparently without establishing a wage with them. At the end of the day, he paid first the workers whom he hired later. He gave them the wage he agreed to pay those who started at the beginning of the day, so those labourers thought they would, therefore, get more. But they did not, so they understandably grumbled. But the reality was that they had come to an agreement with the landowner prior to beginning work, so he was under no moral obligation to pay them more, even if he chose to pay the other labourers the same amount.

I can picture Canada's "Human Rights" Commissioners in the role of the self-righteous religious leaders of the day (the ones who Jesus called "white-washed sepulchres"), vigorously condemning Jesus for violating the "fundamental human rights" of those all-day labourers, and arguing for the state to intervene to retroactively adjust the contractual terms between the landowner and those labourers. These fanatical implementers of their own man-made state religion would have shaken with rage in the face of the moral assumptions Christ was making by using this parable to convey a spiritual truth. Such is the inherent incompatibility between Christian ethics and the morality of Canada's "human rights" industry.

CHAPTER FOUR

DOES THE GOVERNMENT FUNDING OF CHRISTIAN HORIZONS MATTER?

The one aspect of the OHRT decision against Christian Horizons that has generated the most discussion has been the fact that the organization receives almost all its funds from the Ontario government. This is interesting because that wasn't a significant aspect of the decision. It's interesting to see how people's pre-conceived notions in this regard have dominated the discussion among critics.

Canadian conservatives have become used to decisions, particularly in the realm of education, where the government uses its funding of activity as the rationale for imposing its value system on that operation.

Early in this decision, in paragraph 12, the adjudicator acknowledges the government funding of Christian Horizons:

The Commission... perceives the issue in this case as whether an organization which is effectively 100 per cent publicly funded, which provides social services on behalf of the government to the broader community, and offers those services to individuals without regard to their race, creed or cultural background, may discriminate in its hiring policies on the basis of one of the proscribed grounds in the *Code*.

Later on however the adjudicator indicates that this government funding had no bearing on his decision:

[159] I have found that receipt of public funds or support is not determinative of whether an organization may fall within the exemption provided in section 24(1)(a). ... It is not the receipt of public funds *per se*, but an organization's choice to move from the realm where the nature and purpose of its activity is to serve the private interests of its community, into the broader public sector.

Earlier the adjudicator notes:

[116] As to receipt of public funds, again, it is not clear why an organization that receives public funds cannot be a religious organization. ... Section 24(1)(a) may also apply to charitable, philanthropic and fraternal organizations. ... There may well be legitimate public policy discussions and debate about whether an organization that has restrictive membership or employment policies should receive public funds. However, the mere fact that such an organization does receive public funding, even all its funding, does not preclude finding it to be a religious organization, provided other indicia of that status are established on the evidence.

So, in answer to the question "Does the government funding of Christian Horizons matter?" No. The fact that Christian Horizons is funded by the Ontario government is not a determinative factor in this case. But it is important, and the debate around the civil government's funding of charitable work is relevant to Christians who have to evaluate the relative merits of seeking state funds for their work in the days ahead because it is a flashpoint for criticism from certain quarters in our society today as has been evident in the debate on this OHRT decision.

Having said that the government funding of Christian Horizons is not an issue for this case, it is important to note that two other aspects of the intersection of the civil government with Christian Horizons are important to this case, and they will be examined later.

As long as the state is involved in social service work and "charitable" activity, it has two alternative approaches to operating in this sphere. It can micro-manage social service work with comprehensive regulations, including a strict moral code that is to be imposed on all organizations which operate in this sector. Alternatively, it can provide very minimal oversight and regulations, allowing social service and charitable organizations to reflect the diversity of the population in various ways. This diversity might be seen in the way these organizations operate, the nature of their leadership, the kind of employees who they attract and the moral foundations of these various groups.

The Ontario government is taking the former approach. This is consistent with the socialistic mentality that attracts the state to social service work in the first place. It is also consistent with the fact that Secularism is a distinct worldview with its own value system. And it is consistent with the idea that the civil government is expected to be accountable for the taxpayer dollars it hands out.

It is naïve and idealistic to expect the state to operate in the long-term from a "social contract" perspective in which the civil magistrate, without a value base of his own, demonstrates funding flexibility that reflects the religious make-up of the taxpaying public. Secular Humanism has become entrenched in Canada's power centres with opinion-makers insisting that this Secularism represents a morally neutral realm of values around which all people of good will should be able to meet to arrive at a consensus for effectively governing the jurisdiction in question. The practical effect of this deceptive "pluralism" has been to push faithful Christianity out of Canada's public square.

A pragmatic argument that one can make against a micro-managing state is that, although the agent who provides funds to an operation may have a moral right to influence the way the fund recipient works, that agent does not have to do so – and in fact it may be to their advantage not to do so. The adjudicator in this case noted in his decision that government funding of a charity did not inherently preclude that organization from operating according to the dictates of the Christian religion.

Consider an illustration from the business world. A person looking for funds to invest may see a successful business that is looking for more capital to expand. This investor knows that he doesn't have what it takes to make that business successful, but he sees that those who are running it know what they are doing. He may therefore invest his money with them, but he knows that it's best for him not to pursue an active role in the leadership of the company.

Christian Horizons has received government funds (the current funding level is $75 million per year) for decades. They operate 180 group homes. And they have had tremendous success. In fact, the provincial government changed its overall approach to serving disabled people because of the effectiveness of Christian Horizons' group home model. "Christian Horizons is, and has been since 1964, a practical ministry expression of the Evangelical Christian faith," wrote Don Hutchinson, general legal counsel for the Evangelical Fellowship of Canada in an article on this case.

> Over the decades, it has ministered to special-needs children at group homes across Ontario. Christian Horizons' success contributed to the province's decision to close large institutional care facilities and move to a community group-home model for the provision of services for developmentally disabled individuals. As the large institutions closed, Christian Horizons expanded to over 180 residential homes, over 2,500 employees and approximately 1,400 residents. (Hutchinson, 2008)

If the Ontario government was pragmatic, it would leave Christian Horizons alone. The provincial politicians, however, are strident ideologues, so they are expected to force compliance to their value system by Christian Horizons or take over their operation. Sadly, other such organizations in Ontario and across Canada should expect to face similar decisions in the months and years ahead.

The tragedy is that if the Ontario government took over from Christian Horizons, it would necessarily institutionalise and bureaucratise the operation. That's what civil governments do. It's part of their nature. And such a system, regardless of people's intentions, would dehumanize the disabled clients. No doubt this inferior care would cost more.

Too often Christians have also given in to the temptation to institutionalise and depersonalise care for the needy, but historically Christians have demonstrated a disproportionate commitment to personal, humane, non-institutionalised charitable service that preserves the dignity of their patients. That's what the founders of Christian Horizons chose to do. Their successful multi-year track record is evidence of the superiority of this Christian vision.

Who thinks they could do this work as well as Christian Horizons does it? Who thinks they could do it as cost-effectively and as humanely as does Christian Horizons? I haven't seen anybody step up to the plate, least of all the Ontario government itself. The silence is deafening. What would happen if Christian Horizons dropped this ministry in the government's lap?

Statistics on charitable service and financial donations repeatedly show that practising Christians have a superior track record to others. (Brookes, 2006; Ostling, 2007) On the other hand, today's secular humanists talk a lot about human dignity – and they exploit the phrase to advance political agendas such as the homosexuality of the lesbian complainant in this case, Connie Heintz – but they know nothing of the concept.

Listen to this regular columnist in the *Waterloo Region Record*;

> "Over the years, I've seen several local examples where Christian groups suffering from homophobic, evangelical tunnel vision have discriminated against those who don't conform with their rigid views. But I've never seen one given $75 million a year by the Ontario government while continuing to exercise the type of intolerant, hurtful and holier-than-thou beliefs force-fed its employees by the Waterloo Region-based Christian Horizons agency. ...While the agency continues to challenge parts of the

recent ruling made by the human-rights tribunal, perhaps it's time for the government to seek out alternate caregivers and consider reducing or ending financial support for Christian Horizons. (Etherington, 2008)

Well, be my guest, Frank Etherington. Start looking yourself if you feel so provoked by this case. Perhaps nobody has looked because Christian Horizons has such a good track record – and quite likely that track record validates their worldview. Perhaps Mr. Etherington is the ignoramus with the (secular humanist) tunnel vision. Go and find some people who want to do what Christian Horizons is doing and who can demonstrate that they could do the job to the same high standards. Put up or shut up!

A very arrogant letter-writer in the *Waterloo Region Record* wrote a letter in which he obviously thought his questions led to a self-evident response critical of Christian Horizons. On the contrary, his rhetoric simply exposes him as another heartless fundamentalist with no concern for the disabled:

> The recent controversy surrounding the ideology of Christian Horizons raises a number of questions that require attention. We must ask ourselves to what extent such a rigid and intolerant ideology has influenced the everyday policies and procedures that impact on the lives of those that are served by the institution.

Ask away, Robert Lethbridge. They aren't a secret society, and they haven't been around for over 40 years because they have a track record of abuse and incompetence. But I shouldn't interrupt…

> To what extent does such a rigid ideology promote acceptance and tolerance toward others' differences? Encourage a professional environment that accommodates

dissent and new and better informed practices? Confuse institutional conformity with sound clinical practice? Promote healthy sexual development? Prepare young people to protect themselves from sexual exploitation? Discourage children and young people from disclosing sexual abuse because they may view victimization as sin, perhaps leading to feelings of isolation, self-loathing, helplessness, low self-esteem and ongoing abuse? Serve a modern multicultural, multiracial and multi-faith society? … It has been my professional experience that such biased and prejudiced beliefs and views filter into everyday practice whether conscious or not. … (Lethbridge, 2008)

At the end of the day, one should not be surprised at the state wanting to impose its ethical code on those organizations that it funds, and I don't think one can argue that it has no right to do so. This approach is not advantageous to the provincial government, to Canadian culture or to the disabled clients served by Christian Horizons, but it's the logical destructive outcome of state-ist secular humanist political theory.

CHAPTER FIVE

DOES CHRISTIANITY MATTER TO CHRISTIAN HORIZONS?

I found it remarkable the degree to which this decision revolved around the question of the Christian nature of Christian Horizons. At the end of the day, the adjudicator, Michael Gottheil, ruled that Christian Horizons' Christianity was of less value and importance than Connie Heintz's apparent homosexuality. He didn't deny that Christianity was fundamental to how Christian Horizons saw itself, but he did assert that this Christianity was not necessary to Christian Horizons' fundamental work, which he said was social service.

One should probably not be surprised at such a decision. Why would materialists and humanists think that something they can't see, feel or touch would make a difference to the work people do on this earth? Nevertheless, there is a viscerally offensive arrogance at work when an outsider who knows nothing of Christianity claims the right to tell a Christian organization that its faith foundation has no bearing on the nature or quality of their work.

The adjudicator assessed that because Christian Horizons' Christianity is not important enough to its primary work that it had no right to impose a moral code on its employees. Because it had no right to impose a moral code on its employees, doing so was inherently discriminatory, and because that action was inherently discriminatory, Christian Horizons violated Ms. Heintz's human rights by objecting to her homosexuality.

That's all very logical, isn't it? Well, no actually. Those premises don't necessitate the conclusions drawn by the adjudicator and other homosexual activists. But it is a convenient line of reasoning, and homosexualist activists will make their minds jump through whatever hoops are necessary to arrive at the conclusions they want. It's almost as though homosexuality and a fundamentalist veneration of sex as god is the central organising principle for some people's thinking. And they will use whatever bizarre and contorted arguments necessary to exonerate, esteem and exalt homosexuality. Mr. Gottheil acknowledged that the case goes to the "very identity and existence" of Christian Horizons, noted EFC's Don Hutchinson. Mr. Hutchinson added that "in falsely concluding that we should be treated as a garden-variety social-service provider rather than a group engaged in religious ministry, Mr. Gottheil pretzels his way through earlier decisions of human rights tribunals and the courts that would disagree with his conclusion." (Hutchinson, 2008) At any rate, Mr. Gottheil's assertion that Christianity has no necessary relationship with Christian Horizons' service is nothing less than the unacknowledged prejudice of a materialistic or naturalist ideology.

Mr. Gottheil is wrong, and all Christians should affirm the interplay between the material and immaterial realms. God is a personal God and He acts in history. He blesses and curses and He works specially and particularly through His people in this world. The strength and maturity of a Christian's relationship with God directly impacts the nature of his work for God in this world.

Unfortunately, Christians in recent generations have made it easy for the Mr. Gottheils of this world to marginalize Christians by saying that their Christianity is not relevant to the work they do here on earth. We have made it easy to be marginalised in this fashion because we haven't practised Christianity as a worldview. Even today far too many Christians have no interest in exploring the specific Christian principles of family life (although there has been a shift in thinking here in recent years with the popularity of groups such as Focus on the Family). What's the rate of Christian divorces compared with non-Christians? What percentage of Christian youth think that sex outside of marriage is not always wrong? How many Christians think abortion is always wrong?

How many Christians actively explore Scripture to determine the Biblical directives and parameters for our decisions about educating, discipling, training and nurturing our children? How many of us seek Biblical direction for our financial decisions or to determine where, how and what our vocations should be? For many, the only "Christian" thinking they do concerning their work is trying to tell people about salvation. That's wholly inadequate. What about our commitment to a Biblical view of politics, music, entertainment and the arts? Many Christians think that attempts to arrive at a distinctly Christian view of these things is silly because they have never thought along those lines.

With that kind of reductionist thinking in the Church, is it a surprise that worldview secular humanists want to marginalize us and push us into the corners and recesses of society? After all, they have to make room for the comprehensive exercise of their own faith. And that's exactly what happened with the Christian Horizons decision. Mr. Gottheil essentially ruled that secular humanists and professing homosexuals have the right to exercise their values in the public square – the right to practise their beliefs/religion as a worldview – but Christians don't. If we aren't prepared to fight for the right to influence the culture and public life with our Christian principles, then we are fools to think that our theological and cultural enemies are going to freely give that space to us.

Of course the Ontario Human Rights Tribunal went even further by selectively choosing "expert" witnesses who reinforced their own prejudice, namely a Salvation Army employee and a homosexual clergyman. This question of the importance of Christianity to the work of Christian Horizons is not going to be resolved by the testimony of witnesses, but if the human rights commission wants to play this game, you'd think that they would at least feign respectability by producing credible witnesses. There was nothing inherently wrong with the testimony from the Salvation Army employee, who was identified as Mr. John Cobrough, the Territorial Director of Employee Relations for Canada and Bermuda for the Salvation Army. Mr. Cobrough testified to the practise of the Salvation Army when it comes to their criteria for hiring employees, including those involved in "social service activities."

The reality before us here is that the OHRT wants to be able to argue that Christianity allows for more flexibility than Christian Horizons is showing. The heathen "human rights" officials want to be able to tell Christians how to act like Christians which, in this case, supposedly means exercising the flexibility – and non-discrimination – expected of them by these "human rights" officials. Indeed, the adjudicator, after listening to Mr. Cobrough, concluded that "a religious organization that provides a variety of social services in the community can have policies which do not restrict employment to co-religionists." Of course they can. But should they? And if a Christian ethic allows for both the Salvation Army approach and that of Christian Horizons, should an agency of the civil government have the right to interfere in such decisions made by employers and business owners?

In an even more transparent example of the Tribunal's "stacked deck" approach to this case, it called in homosexual activist Brent Hawkes as "the Commission's expert in theology." What more evidence do we need that the OHRC is a ghetto of anti-Christian hatred? Mr. Hawkes is Toronto's most well-known homosexual clergyman. Calling him as an "expert in theology" in this case is like asking a fox for permission to cage your chickens. You can't even call this Tribunal a kangaroo court these days for fear of insulting the kangaroo! The Tribunal wanted to arrive at the position that Christian Horizons' Christianity was irrelevant to its social service work, so it acted accordingly.

The zenith of the Tribunal's audacity and use of convenient witnesses was its choice to use the complainant, Ms. Heintz, as a witness. The unprofessionalism of these OHRT is stunning. They don't even pretend to care about traditional principles of jurisprudence and they relish their demagogic power.

In paragraph 52 of the decision, the adjudicator records that "a number of members and employees of Christian Horizons testified how they saw their work as Christian ministry, and how the work could not be separated from their spiritual beliefs." But he then draws on both the Commission **and Ms. Heintz** as witnesses against their testimony: "While the Commission and Ms. Heintz disputed that religion and spirituality were necessarily infused with the daily tasks of providing residential and support services to the residents, …" I don't know whether you call that conflict of interest or whether you simply call it a shameless example of anti-Christian bigotry, but the self-serving arrogance of including the complainant as a witness against testimony deemed inconvenient by the adjudicator is absolutely stunning.

Nevertheless, the fact is that Christian Horizons' Christianity does matter to its ministry to the disabled; it involves more than just providing a certain atmosphere in which to work. It matters because of the ethics that govern the organisation – ethics that attract people for whom their work is a vocation and a ministry as well as employment. These ethics contribute to the safety and protection of the vulnerable disabled clients. These are the kind of ethics that are listed in Christian Horizons' Lifestyle and Morality Statement. Christian Horizons' Christianity also matters because it forms the basis of immaterial realities such as the faith, hope and love that flow from God through the lives of His people as they serve Him and serve others.

Don Hutchinson wrote:
> Christian service of others is an integral extension of the Evangelical Christian faith. The attempt to sever that link is to misunderstand the nature of religion and undermine the very ethos that undergirds Christian Horizons' expression of care and compassion for others. Ultimately, it serves to undermine the supply of loving ministry to those who

would benefit most from its provision. (Hutchinson, 2008)

Michael Coren, in a *Toronto Sun* article on this OHRT decision, noted how important Christianity is to successful charitable work:

> Without Christian groups and Christian people, the social welfare network of Canada would collapse. This is not hyperbole. Walk along almost any main street and look at the names of the houses, associations and institutes that care for the poor, the abused, the marginalized, irrespective of their gender, race, religion or sexuality. Christian welfare groups tend to be the most successful in dealing with the needy, much of their work is performed by volunteers and most of their money comes from donations. They are motivated by their faith – the same faith that leads them to sign morality statements and not to lie, cheat, be promiscuous or, sorry, engage in homosexual sex. (Coren, 2008)

Research on drug and alcohol rehabilitation services has revealed a success rate of 70 percent for the explicitly Christian ministry, Teen Challenge. This is much higher than the success rates for non-Christian, often government-funded programs.

Despite the superior track record among Christians involved in social service ministry, there are people out there who just hate Christians too much and they are willing to make vulnerable people into human sacrifices to their hatred. The religious fanaticism of secular humanist purists prevents them from allowing Christians to demonstrate their superior results in Canada's public square. They don't care what impact their bigotry has on the vulnerable people being cared for by those Christians. They simply don't care about anything except themselves and their narrow ideological agenda. You see that in Connie Heintz's decision to file this complaint in the first place. You see it in the OHRT decision. You see it in the hateful commentary that has followed in the newspapers. Finally, you see it in the responses from provincial politicians. In this controversy, who is actually showing any compassion for the disabled people who need Christian Horizons' services? It certainly isn't the secular humanists.

There are places where Christians have had to stop serving in their communities because of the hateful agenda of intransigent bigots. Michael Coren noted,

> in California the Salvation Army was forced to close down several inner city missions because officials refused to sign a document approving of homosexuality. … In Britain the Roman Catholic church similarly was obliged to shut the doors of its adoption agency. (Coren, 2008)

With developments like this, homosexual activists and other secular humanists celebrated their victories over society's garbage – Christians. While they partied hard, vulnerable people served by those Christians were left to rot – "The destitute suffered terribly as a consequence," reported Mr. Coren after the Salvation Army closures in California. Such may also be the final outcome of this controversy between the OHRC and Christian Horizons – Ontario's disabled citizens be damned!

Unfortunately, Christian Horizons has decided to discontinue their practice of requiring prospective employees to sign their Lifestyle and Morality Statement even while appealing the rest of the OHRT decision. This statement didn't simply screen out non-Christians, it screened out unsavoury and potentially dangerous workers.

One level-headed letter writer, Thorold Marsaw, published in the *Waterloo Region Record*, commenting on Christian Horizons' use of their Lifestyle and Morality Statement, observed:

> Anyone who has taken the time to have a close look at Christian Horizons... has come away impressed.... **Christian Horizons, which is working with some of this nation's most vulnerable souls, has come to the conviction that its staff must be squeaky clean. I'm sure the families of those dear ones take a lot of comfort in knowing that such is the goal of the organization.** Why would anyone in his right mind try to water down the criteria? (emphasis added) (Marsaw, 2008)

Michael Coren made the same point: "One would have thought that clients of the organization would rather approve of being helped by people who don't lie, cheat, watch porn, drink or run around on their spouses. Not according to our betters in the highly lucrative human rights industry." (Coren, 2008)

Mr. Coren's point could be made even more strongly. Disabled people are among the most vulnerable people in society. If their family members are going to entrust them to the care of others, they want to know as much as is possible that their caregivers are trustworthy. The most important contributor to trustworthiness is solid character. Unfortunately moral barbarians have convinced many in our culture that "private" behaviour does not necessarily translate into public behaviour, so employers like Christian Horizons have no business holding their employees accountable for their private behaviour.

Of course, if deviant behaviour remains private, Christian Horizons will not learn about it, but the fact is that they are identifying their standards and expectations, which puts pressure on people of integrity to honour their word if they sign a Lifestyle and Morality Statement.

The importance of Christian Horizon's values is not simply to make a statement, but because many of them have important implications for people's wider behaviour. Research has demonstrated a link between the viewing of pornography and sexual assault. (Shaw, 2008) We are also seeing a rise in rates of sexual behaviour between teachers and students. (Longenecker, 2008) People in positions of power today still exploit vulnerable people who are in their care. (California Catholic Daily, 2007) A very recent Canadian study – a "landmark" study, according to the *Vancouver Sun* – on the sexual exploitation of children (specifically of street kids and runaways) is noteworthy in this regard. The study reveals that "those with physical or mental health issues" are one of the sub-groups of children who are a greater risk of being targeted by sexual predators. (Bellett, 2008)

If Christian Horizons no longer tells its employees that they have to refrain from using pornography, will that decision increase the risk of Christian Horizons' clients becoming victims of sexually predatory employees? A secular humanist driven by his blind faith will probably say no, but the research-backed response is yes. What will be the impact on the personal security of Christian Horizons' disabled clients if the organization becomes professionally disinterested in their employees' sexual behaviours and relationships? Would you feel safer leaving your disabled family member in the care of Christian Horizons if their employees were no longer bound by their Lifestyle and Morality Statement?

I could also dig in to the solid documentation regarding the higher rates of homosexual victimization compared with heterosexual sexual abuse. Since two to three percent of the population are guilty of 30 percent or more of the cases of child sexual abuse, then even though the actual number of child abuse cases by heterosexuals is much higher, the rate of heterosexual sexual abuse is radically lower. (Clowes and Sonnier, 2005)

All this to say that Christian Horizons' clients have reason to feel less safe than they did before the OHRT ruled against the organization. Any rise in the number of cases of abuse at Christian Horizons should be placed squarely at the feet of the OHRC, who should now be recognized as the enablers of abuse that they are. Consider Ms. Heintz herself? Just think about the way this middle-aged lesbian woman, with the help of Ontario's abuse-enablers, is willing to disregard the well-being of Christian Horizons' disabled clients in order to further her own delusional, fanatically self-centred ego. When you contrast that kind of attitude to the Christianity exemplified at Christian Horizons, you have some idea of the value of screening potential employees for the sake of the disabled clients they serve and, therefore, the importance of the Christian ethic and value system that the leadership has tried to preserve for many years.

The points considered in this chapter make it clear that the Christianity of Christian Horizons is vital to the effectiveness of their service. This Christianity is essential to the values that govern their work; it's important for cultivating the positive, service-oriented environment of their work place; and it's crucial for preserving the level of security they provide for their disabled clients.

CHAPTER SIX

FORCED CONVERSIONS: IF CHRISTIANITY IS UNIMPORTANT, THEN SO IS THE RIGHT TO DISSENT

Never known for its humility or modesty, the Ontario Human Rights Tribunal, along with fining Christian Horizons, has ordered the organization to brainwash its employees and to become a secular humanist evangelist on behalf of the provincial government. Maybe the next step will be requiring Muslims to proselytize on behalf of Hindus!

Some people have said that this OHRT decision has verged on thought control. Sun Media columnist, Christina Blizzard, who is generally conservative in her writings, but no special friend to social conservatives, wrote: "This [decision] comes perilously close to telling people of faith what they may and may not believe. It reinforces fears expressed when same-sex couples won the right to wed that religious institutions that are morally opposed to same-sex marriage would be forced to perform such ceremonies." (Blizzard, 2008)

Specifically, the Tribunal has ordered Christian Horizons to "develop and adopt an anti-discrimination and an anti-harassment policy as well as a human rights training program for all employees and managers within six months from the date of the decision."

In other words, Christian Horizons is forbidden from operating on the basis of Christian principles at any point where those principles conflict with the secular humanist moral code. Not only must Christian Horizons practise this code rather than Christian ethics, it must also propagate these values to its employees.

Lorne Gunter has made clear how tyrannical an attack on the freedom of conscience this is in his column titled "Policing thought in Ontario":

> The commission gave CH six months to "develop and adopt an anti-discrimination and an anti-harassment policy" that complies with Ontario's human rights legislation. Under supervision by the commission, the group must conduct a "review of its employment policies" and demonstrate to the OHRC's satisfaction that its hiring practices comply with Ontario's human rights code. In short, the OHRC ruled that the state's morality code must trump CH's. Worse yet, all CH managers and employees must undergo a "human rights training program," which, of course, is a euphemism for government-approved, state indoctrination aimed at re-educating unacceptable beliefs out of employees' heads. … the OHRC is interested in far more than merely assuring an Ontario government contractee is in compliance with provincial government employment standards. It also wants to stamp out political views at variance with those favoured by the Commission. And that's dangerous, very dangerous. The Ontario government may make Christian

Horizons operate its group homes as it wishes, after all, the government is paying the freight. What it may not do, ever, is demand that CH and its employees think as the government wishes. (Gunter, 2008)

Ontario's three leading political parties are so intellectually barren that none of them is willing to name and shame this outrageous stunt as the fascism that it is. Clearly, we're not going to see this out of control government agency reigned in by today's elected provincial officials.

Thankfully, Christian Horizons is appealing this component of the decision. As I said earlier, it appears that Christians alone are left to defend such values in society, defending the foundational principles of a free and just civilization.

CHAPTER SEVEN

THE DANGEROUS RE-DEFINITION OF "PUBLIC"

One of the most important aspects of the OHRT ruling is the way it uses the word "public." Differences in the way people understand "public" have also been reflected in subsequent commentary about the decision. (In my discussion about government funding (Sec. 4), I mentioned that there were two aspects of the relationship between Christian Horizons and the Ontario government that were of greater relevance to this case. This is the primary aspect to which I was referring.)

There are essentially two definitions of public at play. Confusion between the two makes it easier for cunning individuals and those pushing a revolutionary agenda to advance their cause with little resistance.

When you hear the terms public school, public funds, public programs or public services, what do you think of? What comes to mind? What does public mean in these cases? In these instances "public" means "government." A public school, as opposed to a private school, is a government-funded and government-operated school. Public funds are monies provided by the civil government. Public programs and services are programs and services administered and funded by the civil government.

What is the other use of the term "public?" In this case, it is also used in contrast to what is private, but it encompasses a much larger realm. "Going out in public" might mean going to the mall or for a walk in the park or somewhere that is not private; somewhere beyond the four walls of your home. If something is said to be available to the public, it's understood as generally available to anybody who wants to see it – as opposed to your diary that want to keep private, e.g. for your eyes only or for the eyes of a discrete number of people to whom you give specific permission to view it.

A private school could be understood as public in this respect because it serves a broad range of people. In this respect, home schooling may be the "private" alternative to what is public because it largely takes place among individual families. Within the framework of this second use of "public," a private sector business would be understood as part of the public realm because the general public can walk in to examine your products or solicit your services.

This distinction between the two uses of "public" is incredibly important when discussing a situation such as the Christian Horizons case which is before us. Some people are saying that because Christian Horizons receives government – really taxpayer – funds, it can't complain when the government tells it how to operate.

But it is a wholly different thing to say what the Ontario Human Rights Commission is saying, which is that because Christian Horizons serves the general public (rather than serving only Christians, for example), it must comply with the demands of the civil magistrate.

The first concept – that "public" is synonymous with "government" – captures only those entities that are part of the civil government or regulated by them, such as government departments and Crown Corporations.

This latter notion flows out of a totalitarian, state-ist mentality and is a violent assault on any notion of democratic liberty.

When you use the second definition of "public" outlined above, you are talking about a much larger collection of organizations, in fact, probably the majority of private sector businesses and other bodies – such as Christian Horizons and other community service groups. So, if you are an agent of the state, as is the OHRT, and are using this definition of "public," you are immediately claiming jurisdiction over a huge realm of life broadly understood by Canadians as "private" life, including private-sector businesses. Gone is the traditional, liberty-oriented, Western, Judeo-Christian distinction between public and private. Now we're governed by the state-ist, secularist vision in which the civil government becomes all-pervasive and suffocating, intolerant of any dissent.

Even consistently conservative columnist Lorne Gunter made an error of categories in this regard in his column on the Christian Horizons decision. He wrote:

> To some extent, I accept that when Christian or other belief-driven organizations become subcontractors

for government policy, they cannot object to the state imposing its morality on their operation. He who pays the piper calls the tune. Barbara Hall, the Chief Commissioner of the OHRC, is not entirely wrong, then, when she says 'when faith-based and other organizations move beyond serving the interests of their particular community to serving the general public, the rights of others, including employees, must be respected.' It's insulting to suggest CH does not respect rights when it is operating within its private sphere, but point taken: When CH became an agent of state policy it lost its ability to resist state morality. (Gunter, 2008)

Mr. Gunter is confounding both notions of public. At the beginning and end of this paragraph, he references the notion of Christian Horizons as a recipient of government funds as a legitimate basis for the government requiring compliance with its ethical demands. But in the middle, as though it's part of the same concept, he cites Barbara Hall's statement, which uses the fact that Christian Horizons serves the general public – not the fact of their use of government funds – as her justification for imposing the government's moral demands on the organization.

This is not the first time that this concept of "public" has been used to crush dissent in what used to be treated as part of the realm of private life, where the ethic of maximum liberty reigned. The inherently totalitarian ideology of homosexualism has been used to advance this ethic of socialist tyranny for many years now. Scott Brockie, the private sector businessman, was found guilty of illegitimate discrimination by the OHRT in the mid 1990s because he served the general public, even though he did so as a non-coercive private sector businessman. (Lorne Gunter made the point that even if Christian Horizons was wholly privately funded, he thought the OHRT would have ruled against it anyway, and he used the Brockie case as the precedent for that possible outcome. We have been moving in the direction of comprehensive socialist tyranny for more than a decade now; it will take time, energy and commitment to reverse this trend.)

Public school teacher Chris Kempling has been prosecuted and persecuted for his mildly critical public writings on homosexuality by the BC College of Teachers (BCCT) because he is a public school teacher. Supposedly this public role of his forbids him from sharing his views in public forums outside of the school system. He's never allowed to take off his "public school" hat. So far Mr. Kempling has not met with much success in defending himself against numerous prosecutions by the BCCT and before the BC human rights commission.

There is also the case of Christian Bed & Breakfast owners in Prince Edward Island a few years ago. They refused to rent any of their rooms to a homosexual couple. The homosexuals then threatened to drag these private sector business owners before the province's human rights commission. Instead of suffering through that ordeal, they shut down their business. P.E.I.'s "Conservative" Tourism Minister at the time condemned the private business owners. He claimed that because the B&B business was part of the province's tourism industry, they were obligated to operate under the moral (non-discrimination) framework of the province.

This constant and self-serving manipulation of the lines between private and public by demagogues in Canada is being used to subjugate more and more of Canadian life under the jurisdiction and moral demands of the civil government. This is a tyrannical, state-ist strategy and, in most cases, it is being advanced under the auspices of Canada's homosexual activist movement.

Simply from a pragmatic perspective, requiring an organization to comply with the Human Rights Code because it is serving the general public is bizarre. In effect, the Ontario Human Rights Commission, as an agent of the provincial government, is encouraging organizations that don't subscribe to "Human Rights" to be or remain insular, introverted and self-serving because that's the only way they can operate according to their ethical convictions. Listen to the way adjudicator Michael Gottheil puts it in his decision:

> [158] As I have said, the Legislature has made a policy choice in determining how the rights of a religious organization, and the rights of an individual to be free from discrimination in employment should be balanced. It has determined that where the organization is primarily engaged in serving the interests of its members or its community of co-religionists, it will be granted freedom to restrict hiring to members of its faith, subject to the qualification being reasonable and bona fide. Where, however, it branches out into the public realm, where the nature and primary purpose of its activity creates a relationship with the broader public, its rights are then limited, and, as pertaining to the social activity of employment, it cannot infringe on the fundamental rights of others.

It is purely discretionary for the civil government to use the broad socialistic definition of public in order to capture groups like Christian Horizons in its net. The provincial government, therefore, bears full responsibility for the needless Christian-hating bigotry it is demonstrating with this approach to "human rights" and Christian ministries.

In light of this abusive use of "public," an editorial in the *Waterloo Region Record* asked an interesting question: "The ultimate outcome of the ruling against Christian Horizons could be a series of uncomfortable questions about other religious groups that perform services for the general public. … Will Christian Horizons now decide that the only way it can live up to its Christian beliefs is to cut back on its work and serve only the evangelical Christian community? (Waterloo Region Record, 2008)

The fact is that Christianity is a worldview and the Christian charitable impulse extends beyond the doors of the Church, so Christians would never voluntarily settle for serving only themselves. The shortsightedness of secularist bigotry that could push people in that direction is evidence of a bankrupt ideology.

When did the public park become your bedroom?

There's another aspect of this whole transformation in the notion of public and private that is worth noting here because of its importance to the homosexual movement. Many Canadians are familiar with former Liberal Prime Minister Pierre Trudeau's infamous line, "the state has no business in the bedrooms of the nation." The point behind that statement, of course, was that the state should not treat "bedroom" activity as criminal in nature. A related phrase is: "Whatever is done in private between consenting adults should not be any of the state's business."

With this backdrop in mind, how does one deal with the growing demands of fundamentalist sex worshipers and the homosexualist movement to de-criminalise public sex.

Homosexualist groups in Canada, the U.S. and elsewhere are constantly pushing for the right to have sex in public areas such as washrooms and public parks. In March, news reports indicated that local Amsterdam politicians, in the capital of The Netherlands, were considering a proposal to allow public sex in a large city park, supposedly with provisions such as keeping out of sight of children.

In 2007, Fort Lauderdale, Florida mayor, Jim Naugle, announced a campaign to clamp down on public sex in his jurisdiction because of concerns about such behaviour becoming increasingly reckless without consideration for children. Despite the anti-pedophile nature of his campaign, homosexualist fundamentalists launched a militant hate-filled and vengeful campaign against the mayor that completely ignored the pro-child focus of his efforts to clean up public restrooms.

In Toronto, and no doubt elsewhere, despite the fact that public nudity is a criminal offence, homosexuals during the annual Gay Pride Parade, march through Toronto streets partially and fully naked, and in graphic sexual "clothing" in full view of children and police officers. In fact a homosexual website used to proclaim to homosexuals (and it may still be doing so today) that if they wanted to be naked in public and get away with it, they should join Toronto's Gay Pride Parade.

In effect, what these homosexuals are doing is turning a growing realm of public space into their own bedroom. Sexually deviant behaviour that is not supposed to be prosecuted if "enjoyed" in private by consenting adults is now supposed to be tolerated in public places as well. This is just another example of how the concepts of public and private spheres of life are being twisted and manipulated in order to expand simultaneously the sphere of civil government and the pervasiveness of sexual perversion.

Is Christian Horizons an arm of the state?

The other aspect of Christian Horizons' relationship to the Ontario government that needs to be addressed is brought out in paragraph 12 of the OHRT decision. In that paragraph we read: "The Commission ... perceives the issue in this case as whether an organization which is effectively 100 per cent publicly funded, **which provides social services on behalf of the government to the broader community**, ..." (emphasis added).

Is Christian Horizons really providing its services on behalf of the Ontario government – on behalf of the civil government?

In paragraph 114, we read: "The Commission argues that, while Christian Horizons may be organized around a Christian ethos, it is, in reality, a social service agency, **contracted by the government**, to provide care and support ..." (emphasis added).

That's not exactly the same idea. The statement in paragraph 12 implies that Christian Horizons is essentially an arm of the state – that the state is the initiator of this charity and social service. That's not how Christian Horizons began. That's not how most Christian ministries see themselves, even if they receive taxpayer funds from the civil government. Legally, they are structured as a distinct entity, not as a government department or as a Crown Corporation.

If the Ontario government sees itself as contracting the services of Christian Horizons, that's a different matter. That perspective still allows for the social service organization to be its own entity.

But if the Ontario government does hold to the view reflected in paragraph 12 – that Christian Horizons "provides social services on behalf of the government to the broader community" - that is very consistent with the socialistic mentality and the desire of fascists to "nationalize" all of life under the jurisdiction of the civil government.

And if that's true, then Canadians, Christians in particular, must take note of this fact and of the implications of this view within Canada's political Establishment. If Ontario's politicians see groups that receive taxpayer funds as simply extensions of the state, then it's perfectly natural for them to expect these bodies to comply with the moral dictates of the civil government. And if that's the case, they will always work towards forcing compliance to such standards, even if it requires creative interpretation of the law or the passage of new laws. Christians will not be able to win any comprehensive battles in Canada's culture war without changing people's social and political philosophy and convincing them that fascism is un-Canadian.

CHAPTER EIGHT

WHAT ABOUT CONNIE HEINTZ'S DIGNITY AND MENTAL ANGUISH?

As is always the case with these human rights decisions, a major factor considered by human rights commissioners and adjudicators is the dignity and hurt feelings of the complainant. In fact a list of factors that "human rights" tribunals typically consider when awarding damages, a list that is included in this OHRT decision, includes: humiliation experienced by the complainant, hurt feelings experienced by the complainant, a complainant's loss of self-respect, a complainant's loss of dignity, a complainant's loss of self-esteem, a complainant's loss of confidence, the experience of victimization and vulnerability of the complainant.

When I stop to think about that list, I am stunned. Only a pansy of a man could sit still and accept this kind of situation. How depraved did Canada have to become for fathers and mothers – or even friends and neighbours – in this country to willingly surrender this realm of responsibility to the state?

When the state takes responsibility for the kind of nurture and care and friendship and discipleship that is necessary to help people deal with self-respect, dignity, self-esteem, confidence and vulnerability, then you're standing on the threshold of totalitarianism. When Canadians are willing to allow the civil government to exercise responsibility in these areas, society is in a very bad state – not only because people are abandoning their brotherly and sisterly responsibility to be human with each other, but because the state can't fill the gap. The state is not designed to accomplish the rescue of people's self-respect, dignity, self-esteem and confidence. The state is not a person. To throw someone at the state to receive help in these areas is to treat such people as less than human. This secular humanist approach to life is dehumanising and debasing. It destroys human dignity and crushes self-esteem.

The only benefit of this strategy is for cunning tyrants to exact revenge on their enemies, using the power of an irresistible state to intimidate and steal from their opponents. That is exactly what Connie Heintz has done to Christian Horizons through her enabler, the Ontario Human Rights Tribunal. The solution to loss of dignity, to a crushed spirit and to despair is a wad of cash! It might be if the phony victim is a crass, exploitative thug. But to a person genuinely suffering with such brokenness, an offer of money would be spurned as a cold and insensitive gesture by someone who wanted to try to solve the problem quickly because she didn't want to invest the time and effort necessary in another person to bring real healing.

So, we know exactly where Connie Heintz has positioned herself. It's unfortunate that Michael Gottheil, the adjudicator in this case, lacked the heart, the compassion and the appreciation for human dignity to address this case respectfully and intelligently.

So what exactly did Mr. Gottheil think he discovered about Ms. Heintz in the course of his OHRT investigation?

In paragraph 263, he wrote: "…the fact remains the feelings of vulnerability, isolation, self doubt, loss of dignity and emotional exhaustion experienced by Ms. Heintz were tied to her experience as a gay person in an environment that was anti-gay, and, as a result of an investigation process, which was tainted and targeted against her…"

From paragraph 11: "For Ms. Heintz, this case is equally fundamental. It is tied to her identity and dignity, to her sexuality, to her sense as a person of faith."

From paragraph 85: "On September 22, 2000, Ms. Heintz resigned from her employment with Christian Horizons. … but felt that the stress and the environment at work was not bearable. She felt the staff and co-workers at Christian Horizons thought she was 'scum and dirt' and did not treat her 'like a human being'."

From paragraph 268: "… As a result of the extreme emotional anxiety she suffered as a result of her treatment by Christian Horizons she concluded she was unable to continue working in her chosen field."

And from paragraph 255: "I award… $5000.00 for mental anguish caused by actions that were wilful and reckless."

The fact that these are relevant points in an investigation by the civil government is astounding. Our forefathers would throw us all back into diapers and stuff soothers in our mouths.

There are other particulars of this case and the way Ms. Heintz was treated so deferentially that are deeply troubling.

Firstly, there is the prejudice of secular humanism that a person's sexual thoughts and behaviour is fundamental to a person's identity and dignity. This is such a base and degrading view of humanity. The reality is that this inferior view of man was popularised by the homosexual political movement and revolves around the rhetoric of "sexual orientation." But it's just as base to consider a healthy view of sexuality as fundamental to human dignity. In fact, those with a healthy view of sexuality don't treat sex as a vital component of human dignity.

But in this case, Ms. Heintz's sexuality – because she claimed to be a lesbian – was predictably treated as more fundamental to who she was than Christian Horizons' Christianity was to that organization, and the adjudicator was, of course, very affirming towards how Ms. Heintz viewed her sexual self.

In paragraph 4, we read: "Ms. Heintz is an individual of deep Christian faith. She is also a lesbian. Ms. Heintz **came to an understanding of who she was, and her sexual orientation** during her tenure as an employee of Christian Horizons" (emphasis added). The adjudicator allows Ms. Heintz to be simultaneously a woman of "deep Christian faith" and a lesbian. He also equates her discovery of who she was with her decision to start surrendering to homosexual lust. What a degrading view of humanity!

In paragraph 251, the adjudicator writes:

> On a personal level, for Ms. Heintz, the effect of the discriminatory policy was to say to her, because of who you are, you are no longer welcome. Ms. Heintz worked for Christian Horizons for five years. She was dedicated to her work and the individuals she supported. She was a valued employee and a full member of the Christian Horizons "community." The effect of the policy was to make her a pariah within the organization and force her to leave her employment. Her years of education, hard work and commitment were all unimportant in comparison to her sexual orientation. The policy was a fundamental affront to Ms. Heintz's dignity and self-respect.

In at least a couple of places the adjudicator acknowledged that while some people – e.g. Christians – might still deem homosexuality to be wrong and immoral, this is not the position of Canadian law. The reality is that the law is moral and both the law and the adjudicator make clear moral statements, not simply legal statements. And those moral statements demand conformity to anti-Christian homosexuality-affirming ethics. A case in point is paragraph 256 where he says:

> I find this violation to be particularly serious and deserving of a substantial damage award for several reasons. First, I have found that Christian Horizons failed completely to ensure that its workplace environment was free from discrimination against gays and lesbian. **Its policy, based on the belief that homosexuality was unnatural and immoral, engendered fear, ignorance, hatred and suspicion. It sent the message to employees that gays and lesbians were not equal members of the workplace community** (emphasis added).

Of course, these values are antithetical to Christian ethics, and the two can never be reconciled. All non-marital sexual activity is wrong; it's sinful. And, therefore, when a person gives in to temptations to engage in such activity, it is at those times that they attack their own dignity. Their dignity does not suffer when people call them to account and challenge them for their sinful, destructive behaviour. That such an attitude is protected, rather than challenged, by Canada's cultural Establishment today is evidence of moral degradation and the incompatibility of the "human rights" ethic with authentic Christianity.

And, in a stark example of hypocrisy, Mr. Gottheil also condemned Christian Horizons' attempt to counsel Ms. Heintz. In paragraph 209, he writes:

> I have no doubt that Christian Horizons' intention in providing spiritual counselling to employees generally, is to support individuals it considers members of its religious community. In this context, counselling is offered in a caring and compassionate way. But the attempt of "restoration" for persons who are gay or lesbian is profoundly disrespectful and oppressive. Notwithstanding that Christian Horizons sincerely believes that homosexuality is unnatural and immoral, homosexuality is neither a crime nor an illness. Gays and lesbians are entitled to be treated by their employers, even where those employers may be religious organizations, with respect and dignity, and not be offered counselling to cure them of their sexuality.

Why is this hypocritical? Because a key aspect of this case, to Mr. Gottheil, is the fact that Christian Horizons serves the general public, not just Christians, and that is why it is not permitted to demand Christian standards from its employees. But in an example of the Christian organization attempting to act Christianly to a professing Christian employee, it still gets chastened. The moral of this story is that when Big Brother has you in his scope, it's almost impossible to get away without a bullet in your head!

And where are Mr. Gottheil's credentials as a sex therapist? His patronizing tone towards Christian Horizons – I'm sure they had good intentions! – is bad enough, but he also asserts as a statement of fact that it is "disrespectful" and "oppressive" to try to restore someone enslaved in sexual sin. But of course that is an ideological and religious statement, flowing from the view that homosexuality is an "identity" issue. It is wholly incompatible with any serious view of science or human nature.

In several places, Mr. Gottheil acknowledged that Christian Horizons officials treated Mr. Heintz with respect and sought to help her find new employment rather than kicking her out at the first opportunity. But Mr. Gottheil's concern is ideological, not human, so in the final analysis he ruled that Christian Horizons' actions where "wilful and reckless" because of the fact that the conflict between both parties revolved around Ms. Heintz's homosexuality. And elsewhere (paragraph 211), the adjudicator writes: "In my view, the evidence demonstrates a clear animus against Ms. Heintz by Christian Horizons' management from the point at which the organization discovered she was lesbian, and in a same-sex relationship."

Having said all this, there was also extensive coverage given in the decision to an investigation of Christian Horizons' claims and records related to interpersonal conflicts among staff involving Ms. Heintz as well as at least one accusation of abuse of a disabled client. As is probably the case in most organizations that don't have the resources to operate "clinically" 100 percent of the time, the adjudicator found a number of examples of conflicting information and a failure of leaders to follow-through with investigations and to follow protocol perfectly. This adjudicator, pretending to be God, likes to think that he can, several years after the fact, enter into these experiences sufficiently to make reliable judgments about what transpired.

In a real court of law, with cases like this where there is too much conflicting testimony, the evidence is typically thrown out. But not in a kangaroo court! "Human rights" adjudicators like situations such as this because they get to pretend they are master detectives, and the lack of clarity enables them to spin the material however they choose, which is typically in favour of the complainant. Needless to say, none of this material that raised questions about Ms. Heintz's integrity and credibility was used against her by Mr. Gottheil.

Speaking of the preferential treatment and open favouritism shown to the complainant, one of the most hideous parts of the decision is found in paragraph 285. Listen to this:

> No later than six months from the date of this decision, Christian Horizons shall submit a report to the Tribunal outlining the steps it proposes to take, along with a time frame for implementation, to ensure that its employment policies are in compliance with the *Code*. At least 30 days prior to the submission, Christian Horizons shall provide its proposal **to the Commission and Ms. Heintz**, and the Commission and Ms. Heintz shall be entitled to make submissions to the Tribunal on the proposal. Any agreement reached between the parties should be identified in a joint submission. Following receipt of the proposal and submissions, the Tribunal will provide

directions for a process to finalize the award in this case (emphasis added).

Did you catch that? Well of course you did because I bolded it. I still can't believe what I'm reading. The concept of restitution is one thing, but to require the defendant to produce a resolution that the complainant is allowed to vet, makes the complainant also an adjudicator; it gives the complainant a position of authority over the defendant. This kind of stunt must violate a conflict of interest principle somewhere. Furthermore, Ms. Heintz is not an "expert" in this field, so there's a stark lack of professionalism in a practise that allows her to have a say over the acceptability of the defendant's compliance with the orders.

Giving Ms. Heintz this kind of authority in this case is so thoroughly offensive that the only image I could find to convey its revulsion was that of grinding a dog's nose in its own vomit. This kind of tactic by adjudicator Gottheil is an act of gross humiliation of the defendant. It's degrading, humiliating and dehumanising. If Christian convictions against homosexuality are an expression of hate, then this stunt is evidence that the OHRC is a fascist torture chamber. Whatever it is, it is wholly incompatible with a free and democratic society.

There was another part of this decision that sent shivers up my spine because of the arrogance Mr. Gottheil betrayed in his "god-play" as a representative of the civil government. In paragraph 252 we read:

> I would have awarded a greater level of general damages for the violation of Ms. Heintz's rights occasioned by the application of the policy, but I find that part of the stress Ms. Heintz experienced arose from her own crisis of faith. Ms. Heintz testified that when she joined the organization,

she had no difficulty signing the Lifestyle and Morality Statement because it reflected her own beliefs. She lived by and in accordance with the Doctrinal Statement and the Lifestyle and Morality Statement until late in 1999. She testified that when she began to gain an understanding of her sexuality and sexual orientation, it was a "complete dichotomy shift" and "a complete struggle."

Where does a fellow human being get off thinking that he has the right, let alone the ability, to parse such complex and confusing dynamics in order to arrive at a punishment for somebody who supposedly caused harm to the complainant in such a context? The fact that the state in Canada has these powers is terrifying. I feel like I live in a Gestapo compound. Who is really safe in a political environment like this?

Ms. Heintz should be sent packing and told to get on with life as a productive human being. But no… this self-centered, vengeful woman is enabled by the OHRT to exact her revenge on Christian Horizons. And we know it's revenge because the adjudicator made it clear that she has no interest in returning to work at Christian Horizons. She filed this complaint because "she seeks validation of the wrong she perceives to have been done to her, and recognition as an equal human being" (paragraph 11).

"Seeks validation of the wrong" is a euphemism for revenge. The state should suppress revenge. Revenge is far more likely to result in violence and murder than anything the political left calls "hate." But instead of suppressing revenge, human rights commissions become the enablers of revenge. For this reason alone, a just government would treat human rights commissions as criminal organizations.

Not surprisingly, when Ms. Heintz was contacted by a newspaper following the announcement of Christian Horizons' intention to appeal part of the decision, her response was purely ideological and clinical. She's not suffering from any loss of dignity or mental anguish. In the *Waterloo Region Record* we read:

> Heintz, reached last night, was not relishing the prospect of another prolonged court battle. "It's been seven years," she said. "This is a never-ending story." The decision to drop the lifestyle contract is "one small victory," she said, but Heintz is frustrated that public funds may cover the group's ongoing legal bills. "I think they're appealing because they can," she said. "Unfortunately, Christian Horizons is taking taxpayers' money to support this." (Mercer, 2008)

Arrogance must be bliss! Ms. Heintz can object to the use of taxpayer dollars by Christian Horizons to appeal the OHRT decision, but she has expressed no remorse over her use of taxpayer dollars to persecute Christian Horizons in the first place.

CHAPTER NINE

BREAKING THE BACKS OF THE CHURCHES?

Having moved as far as they have now, when will Canada's civil government agents and homosexual activists throw their noose around the neck of the Church itself, of Christian congregations as they worship God in the supposed privacy of their own sanctuaries?

The Canadian Council of Christian charities has already been counseling churches on how to structure their mission statements and other official documents and how to function in order to best protect themselves in the face of possible charges of discrimination. This typically involves activity beyond the regular worship of those churches, particularly in larger churches that may provide direct oversight over other activities, in particular those that involve the hiring of employees, such as child care services or seniors care centres.

When it came to the controversy over changing the definition of marriage to embrace homosexual relationships, the federal Liberal government said that it was committed to protecting religious freedom. It turned out that it was only willing to protect the "religious" freedom of clergy. Marriage commissioners, solemnizing marriages on behalf of the state in most provinces are required to perform same-sex ceremonies when requested, or their application to be a marriage commissioner will not be accepted. In Saskatchewan, a marriage commissioner is facing a human rights complaint from homosexuals whom he refused to "marry."

In addition, the religious freedoms of others in the marriage industry, such as photographers, cake decorators, caterers, etc., are not protected. If such people refuse to serve homosexual couples, they risk facing human rights complaints. A Knights of Columbus branch in B.C. faced a human rights inquisition in 2005 over their refusal to allow lesbians to use their facilities for a "wedding" reception.

In the face of this controversy over the definition of marriage, a clergyman publicly argued that Christians shouldn't have the right to use "religious liberty" as a shield for discriminatory actions. The clergyman was renegade, pro-homosexual Anglican bishop, Michael Ingham of Vancouver. But he's still a clergyman and agenda-driven secularists don't care whether or not he's considered a rebel by other Christians. They will still exploit his dissent to advance their own homosexual Fundamentalist agenda. Mr. Ingham's actual words were: "I've always been distressed by arguments for religious people to be able to continue to discriminate against gay and lesbian people. I don't believe in that kind of God. It's as if one is saying, "If you're a non-believer, you can't discriminate. But if you're a believer you can"." (Harvey, 2004)

The reality is that there is no such thing as a constitutionally secure freedom of religion in Canada. Almost every time that practitioners of homosexuality butt heads with Christians, especially in courts and human rights commissions, Christians and Christian ethics are forced to give way to the absolute right of (homo)sexual license.

So, what's the next move for Canada's (homo-)secularist Establishment? What is there left for them to do to finish their job of criminalizing Christianity? Selecting our pastors? Vetting sermons and Sunday School curriculum? Restricting the size of church facilities? Perhaps, but most likely the next move will be an attempt to revoke the Church's charitable tax status. There has already been talk and some investigation into moves in that direction in recent years. Most recently, a proposal to restrict the tax exemption for religious facilities was included in a leaked document to be considered by the City of Brampton, Ontario. "Among other things, that policy paper suggest[ed] that all 'places of worship' should start paying property taxes on everything but the specific places where the worship is held. In the case of churches, that would make offices, nurseries, fellowship halls, and parking lots subject to property taxes," reported No Apologies at the time. (Siebring, 2008)

Christians hold to a range of views as to the legitimacy and value of churches possessing charitable tax status. I won't explore the various views here. The point is that in our particular context, moves in this direction reflect hostility towards the Church and Christianity by Canada's secularist Establishment. They don't flow out of a principled view of the need to sever this example of the state's implicit control over the church. They reflect hostility towards Christianity.

As a practical point, without the charitable tax credit, many, if not most, churches would experience a drop-off in giving that would have a not inconsequential impact on their budgets. We can argue among ourselves whether that would be a useful purifying force in Canada's Church but at least in the short-term, I expect that such a move will not be helpful to the influence of the Church in Canadian culture. Churches should anticipate and prepare for this change to Canada's tax laws, perhaps by providing more teaching on tithing, as well as teaching on the comprehensive scope of true discipleship – discipling the nations. Some teaching on Christianity as a worldview wouldn't hurt either, including Biblical political theory and the nature of the relationships between the Church, the state, the family, economic activity and self-government. Mentorship in faithfulness wouldn't hurt either.

I'll close this chapter with an extended citation from *Calgary Herald* columnist Nigel Hannaford's presentation of a possible scenario for the days ahead:

> I don't think the church generally has appreciated that the state has no obligation to give it a property-tax break or make tithes tax-deductible, if the church preaches a message the state doesn't like. Which, in times past, it often has.

> Long before there were tax breaks, the church did good work out of love for God. The first hospitals, schools and universities were founded hundreds of years ago by the church. As this was to the state's advantage, it gave the church concessions. This, too, was logical: why make it more difficult for somebody caring for the sick by taxing his hospital?

But those were different days. In Christendom, even men who rejected Christ for themselves nonetheless acknowledged His church as the source of morality.

Today's consensus places equality above biblical teachings as the supreme moral virtue. Indeed, for mankind's greater comfort, the very concept of sin has been banished and this OHRC decision is a case in point. For it does not merely find Christian Missions discriminated against a lesbian employee by insisting on its moral code. It says the moral code must go – AND goes on to tell the mission what it must think: out with Scripture and in with contemporary understandings of human rights. Our moral code is better than your moral code, believe it.

This has disturbing, oppressive overtones. The day is coming when the church, as an institution, will have to decide which it will serve. (For Christian Horizons, that day is here.)

Loss of tax privileges would grievously hurt its ability to serve the community. Yet, the church's first duty is to be faithful to God's word – service is a consequence of that, not the church's prime function – and that may come at a price. Didn't it always, though? The quicker the church weans itself off tax privileges, the quicker it will be strengthened to resist the state when the state intrudes on its doctrine.

Caesar is welcome to his tax, but not to worship. (Hannaford, 2008)

WHAT'S A CHRISTIAN TO DO IN THIS HOSTILE ENVIRONMENT?

That's the million-dollar question: What's a Canadian Christian to do in the face of this growing hostility to, and criminalization of, our faith?

First of all, we must maintain the right posture.

We're winners.

Or we're losers! I've been looking for some middle ground, and I just can't find any!

If you're not sure whether you want to win this culture war, you're not going to be fired by the faith and vision necessary to win against today's human rights commission onslaught, not to mention the rest of the secular humanist army that's marching, jackboot-clad, across this country.

Unfortunately, many Christians get queasy when people talk about winning. Probably, much of that is over the perceived incompatibility between humility and wanting to win.

Christians should stop viewing defeat as a sign of humility, and winning as a sign of pride. Jesus didn't play tiddlywinks with Satan; He kicked him in the teeth and crushed his neck. And Satan will be forced against his will to bow before Christ and acknowledge His Lordship and sovereignty. So will all God's enemies. Christ is a conquering King. That's not all He is, but it's a big part of who He is. And we share in that victory. If we shrink from this, God will discipline His Church with defeat in the culture wars.

I think many Christians also avoid the concept of winning because they see it as selfish – that Christians, like everyone else, are only concerned about winning in order to gain the upper hand on everyone else. That is nonsense, at least among those who think rightly about winning.

I want to win for the glory of God. I want to win to see God's justice and mercy spread across Canada. I want to win to see government policy put in place that rewards industry and integrity, not laziness and dishonesty. This means the elimination of redistributive taxation policies and a severe contraction in social welfare policies, if not the elimination of such – so that hard-working families that are committed to hard work and planning a future for their children, people who sacrifice for others, are rewarded, not punished. And this means forcing indolent people to be confronted with the results of their dishonesty and laziness sooner rather than later when their condition could be far worse.

I want to win to implement public policies that do not subsidize and promote sexual promiscuity. Not for some academic, theoretical reason but because sexual promiscuity is the source of the long-term misery of low-income single parenthood, it's the source of rising rates of infertility, it's the source of our genocide against unborn children.

When Christians win, everybody wins – except criminals and parasites. That's the promise of Scripture and it's the testimony of history.

Practically speaking, this means that we need more Christians in positions of leadership in our culture – in education, media, civil government and elsewhere.

But Christianity is not a religion of revolution, so in order to see more Christians rise to positions of leadership and influence, they need to get there through civil and democratic means. This means working hard, being involved in public life at different levels, volunteerism and community service – service, service, service. It means having a reputation for excellence, recognition among your peers, and expanding your sphere of influence. And, to gain political office, you must use the democratic process that is in place in our country.

No, we're not going to regain the upper hand in our culture overnight. God wouldn't humiliate Himself by giving us such victory overnight because leadership requires character and God knows that most of us don't have the character necessary to lead. Character is forged in conflict. It's easy to be a loser. All you have to do is sit there and look stupid. But victory is born of courage and sacrifice and resolve and service.

Christians committed to discipleship, especially when it comes to the rearing of their own children, will be Christians of vision, Christians who can shape their children with a spirit of victory. So, let's be people who want to win. If we aren't, we'll lose and life will be far more miserable for our children than it is for us. That's not what you want for your children and it's not what you want as your legacy. (Cf. Psalm 103:17; Proverbs 13: 22 and Ezekiel 37:25.)

Practically speaking, many Christians think they can make peace with their enemies, particularly the dominant secularists of our day. I hope I have shown here how hostile and dangerous Secularism is to civil society and to Christianity. If not, I urge you to read my book, "State vs. Church: What Christians Can Do to Save Canada from Liberal Tyranny." I lay out very clearly how Secularism is a distinct and dangerous totalitarian religion that is committed to the destruction of the democratic tradition that Christianity brought to the world through what we often call Christendom and Western civilization.

Many people today still think or pretend that Secularism is firstly democratic and freedom-minded and, secondly, that it represents a realm of moral neutrality and rational pluralistic compromise. So, for example, we often hear people recommending that countries suffering under an Islamic theocracy would be better off if they adopted a secular approach to government. Nothing could be further from the truth. Secular is just as tyrannical and oppressive. Canada's human rights commissions bear ample testimony to that fact.

What we need is Christian governments and the Christian legacy of democratic governance, sphere sovereignty, equality, the rule of law and a broad space for individual liberty and civil-social freedoms. Today's revisionists claim those principles as part of the legacy of Secularism. That is a massive fraud. And Christians need to be educated and bold enough to declare it so, and to be able to show how these treasured components of a free and just society are rooted in a Christian vision. That is another reason why Christians need to pursue victory. Détente is not a Christian option.

Christians must pray.

The battle is the Lord's. And our battle plan must not depend on "horses and chariots." The Bible doesn't say that we are not permitted to use "horses and chariots." It says that we must not put our trust in them.

We must pray. But we need to pray right. We need to pray expecting results – and expecting the right results. We can't force God's hand anyway, so if we pray amiss, God won't answer the prayer as we would wish, so pray boldly for what you believe is God's will, and if you are not praying right, then God will sort out your thinking "on the fly." It's easier to steer a moving car than one that's locked in park.

Pray for victory. Yes, this also means praying for the defeat of our enemies. We can let God work out the details of that, but we even have examples in the Bible of godly people praying for the destruction of their enemies. Whether God destroys them as enemies by converting them and making them our brothers or sisters, or whether He destroys their work by confounding their minds or confusing their speech, or whether He implements more drastic measures, God does judge in history. And He does so for His glory and for the protection of His people. In Psalm 3, David urges God to break the teeth of His enemies. In Psalm 109, among other things, the Psalmist asks God to visit His enemy with the curses that His enemy was pronouncing against him (v. 17). The Psalms are a hymnbook. When people sing Psalm 136, they are singing thanksgiving to God for drowning the Egyptians as they were pursuing God's people (vs. 13-15).

Pray for mercy. Pray for salvation for unbelievers. Pray for restoration and healing. But also pray for the advancement of the Kingdom of King Jesus. Pray for victory. Pray that God would protect His people by whatever means please Him. When people come against God's Church as viciously as the Ontario Human Rights Commission has attacked Christian Horizons, and as harmfully as they and other human rights commissions have persecuted other Christians – and the Christian truth they represent – then Christians should plead to God for justice and vindication as well as for grace.

Christians also need to be informed.

Christian cannot afford to be surprised by the latest assault on their faith, or the latest attack on another Christian brother. We have an obligation to be informed and up-to-date in what is going on in our culture. If we are engaged, if we are actively sharing our faith with our friends and neighbours in an intelligent manner; which in part means knowing them and their experiences enough to be able to share Christ in a way that is personal for them rather than as an abstract idea, then we would have some idea of what's going on "out there." We can't hide behind the walls of our house and church. We can't bury ourselves in The Sports Network or our favourite Soap Opera or Reality Show.

The focus of this short booklet is a single ruling by the Ontario Human Rights Commission against Christian Horizons. I made passing reference to several other decisions from the past decade. But there are a host of offensive and outrageous decisions and threats from human rights commissions across this country that have been used to push Christians into the closet. These decisions give wider freedom to those whose desires and goals do not contribute or the preservation of decency or genuine freedom in Canada. The worst cases for Christians have been from complaints filed by homosexual activists. Today Mohammedans are jumping on the bandwagon of success experienced by these homosexual activists.

In British Columbia, there have been human rights commission prosecutions and BC College of Teachers prosecutions against Chris Kempling as noted earlier. Also, the Christian Heritage Party – a political party – is facing several "human rights" complaints. Anybody who can't appreciate the threat to fundamental liberties when a political party can be prosecuted for hate crimes has no understanding of the importance and nature of genuine liberty. Also in BC was the case of the Knights of Columbus hall that faced a complaint from lesbians for refusing them use of the hall for their "wedding" reception.

In Alberta, Catholic Bishop Fred Henry faced complaints from homosexual activists and Rev. Stephen Boissoin lost a case brought by a teacher for comments he made against homosexuality in a letter to the editor of a newspaper. And in Alberta, a homosexual complaint against King's College, a Christian institution, resulted in "sexual orientation" being added to that province's human rights code to enable people to launch the kind of complaints that Rev. Boissoin later faced.

In Saskatchewan, Hugh Owens was prosecuted for an ad he had published in a newspaper using Scripture verses to argue against homosexuality. He lost before Saskatchewan's

Human Rights Commission, but later won a rare victory in an appeal in the province's real court system.

In Ontario and Prince Edward Island, we have the Scott Brockie case and the Christian Bed & Breakfast case mentioned above.

Today, Jewish conservative lawyer, journalist, author and pundit Ezra Levant has faced "human rights" complaints from Muslims wanting to smother his and our free speech when it's critical of Islam. Canada's national newsmagazine, *Maclean's*, is, of this writing, facing two "human rights" complaints from Muslims because of content they published by columnist and author Mark Steyn that was sharply critical of Islam.

I could keep going with other examples from Canada' human rights commissions as well as from other sources of persecution such as Canada's media censorship agencies. Most Christians are oblivious to these and other acts of terror against Christianity and against Christian principles such as freedom of speech and freedom of conscience in this land. Educate yourself. If you don't learn now, you'll have lots of time to read later sitting in a prison cell or on the unemployment line as you face your persecution. One of the best ways to keep up to date specifically on the antics of human rights commissions is to regularly read Ezra Levant's blog at *www.ezralevant.com*. To gain access to news links and commentary that keep you up to date on a wider scope of the culture wars in Canada and elsewhere, you can sign up to my newsletter at *www.christiangovernment.ca*. There are other useful "social conservative" resources out there too. I link to some of them on the Links page on my website.

Christians have to be worldview Christians.

This is the assumption of much of what I have said so far in this call to action. In these anti-Christian decisions from human rights commissions, we see Secular Humanism being granted the right to exercise their faith as a worldview, while Christians are being denied access to Canada's public square to make arguments for the value of Christian truth in Canada's public space. Some Christians are willing to settle for this reductionistic, pietistic redefinition of their faith. What a tragedy – not just for Christians, but also for all those vulnerable and weak people in our culture who depend on Christian morality and Christian charity to protect their dignity and their lives from abortionists, euthanasia supporters, thieves, sexual violators and other ruthless and merciless people.

There are a growing number of valuable worldview resources as Christians re-discover this need for a worldview perspective. Focus on the Family's *www.thetruthproject.org* is just one such resource. An internet search will reveal many more.

Christians must live by example.

Don't give state-ists an excuse to justify their oppressive aspirations. Christians must be examples of integrity, industry, charity, thrift, personal responsibility – self-government. "The fruit of the Spirit is love, joy, peace, patience, kindness, goodness, faithfulness, gentleness and self-control" (Galatians 5:22-23).

A primary reason that non-Christians feel comfortable persecuting Christians today is that Christianity is only an academic, theoretical concept to them. They don't know any Christians (or don't know anybody who they know is a Christian). Homosexuals insist that if only Christians would get to know them, we wouldn't see a need to continue fighting homosexuality. That dynamic often works – unfortunately in that respect. But Christians should expand their networks and build relationships with more people, so that more non-Christians in positions of influence will get to know Christians who are decent, noble, charitable, sacrificial, relatively normal, funny, intelligent people. Then these people may be less likely to succumb to the false and negative stereotypes of what Christianity looks like, stereotypes that make it easy for them to make the intolerant decisions against us that we see throughout Canadian courts and human rights commissions today.

You must also contact politicians urging them to abolish Canada's HRCs.

Some Christians today are still playing games, pretending that there is some merit to these HRCs, if only they returned to their original function. There is nothing redeemable in human rights commissions or their mandates or the "human rights" legislation that they are supposed to enforce. Nothing! Unite with a credible position in favour of abolishing them. Contact the federal government to object to the Canadian HRC. Contact your provincial government to demand an end to that province's human rights commission.

I think the following passage from Proverbs aptly summarises the duty of justice and mercy that God has given to Christians. It's a public duty. It's a "get your hands dirty" duty. And it's a duty with a warning because God expects obedience since He has promised us the strength and faith to obey. Let's take

God at His word and prove His faithfulness. Let's stand up and be counted. The clients at Christian Horizons are but one small group of people who will benefit from Christian victory in Canada.

> Rescue those being led away to death;
>   hold back those staggering toward slaughter.
>
> If you say, "But we knew nothing about this,"
>   does not he who weighs the heart perceive it?
> Does not he who guards your life know it?
>   Will he not repay each person according to
>   what he has done?
>
> *– Proverbs 24:11-12*

REFERENCES

Mercer, Greg. 2008. "Employer ordered to compensate fired gay worker, abolish code of conduct." *The Kitchener Record*, April 24.

Hutchinson, Don. 2008. "You can't take the mission out of Christian Horizons." *National Post*, April 29.

Wente, Margaret. 2008. "We're not poor little Indians." *The Globe & Mail*, May 1.

McQuire, Alexander. 2008. "No place in democracy." *Waterloo Region Record*, April 29.

Brooks, Prof. Arthur C. Nov. 27, 2006. *Who Really Cares: The Surprising Truth About Compasionate Conservatism Who Gives, Who Doesn't, and Why It Matters*. Basic Books.

Ostling, Richard N. 2007. "Christianity undergoes global shift, believers outshine secularists on charity." Jan. 3.

Etherington, Frank. 2008. "Government-sponsored agencies shouldn't have a religious bias." *Waterloo Region Record*, May 8.

Lethbridge, Robert. 2008. "Ideological questions." *Waterloo Region Record*, May 1.

Marsaw, Thorold. 2008. "Code of conduct was a good thing." *Brantford Expositor*, April 28.

Coren, Michael. 2008. "Disabling charity." *The Toronto Sun*, May 3.

Crouse, Ph.D., Janice Shaw. 2008. "Pornography and Sex Trafficking: Pornography, prostitution and sex trafficking; linked together in a $4 billion industry." *Concerned Women for America*, May 19.

Longenecker, Rev. Dwight. 2008. "The Epidemic of School Sex Abuse." April 29.

2007. "Sexual abuse of public school students more widespread than parents think." *California Catholic Daily*, November 12.

Bellett, Gerry. 2008. "Landmark sex exploitation study finds surprising number of female abusers." *Vancouver Sun*, May 28.

Clowes, Brian W. and Sonnier David L. 2005. "Child Molestation by homosexuals and heterosexuals." May.

Blizzard, Christina. 2008. "Rights work goes wrong." *The London Free Press*, May 7.

Gunter, Lorne. 2008. "Policing thought in Ontario." *National Post*, April 28.

2008. "Tribunal ruling raises questions." *Waterloo Region Record*, April 28.

Mercer, Greg. 2008. "Christian Horizons drops 'lifestyle and morality' code for employees." *Waterloo Region Record*, May 7.

Harvey, Bob. 2004. "Churches at odds over issue." *The Kingston Whig-Standard*, December 10.

Siebring, Al. 2008. "Brampton Plan Suggests Limiting Number of Churches." *No Apologies Daily News*, January 3.

Hannaford, Nigel. 2008. "Church must decide which it serves: the state or God." *Calgary Herald*, May 3.